this book
belongs to:

_____

_____

First published in France under the title *Les Petits Délices à Partager* © Editions du Seuil, 1997.

Translated by Alexandra M. Childs

Published in 1997 and distributed in the U.S. by
Stewart, Tabori & Chang,
a division of U.S. Media Holdings, Inc.
115 West 18th Street, New York, NY 10011

Distributed in Canada by
General Publishing Company Ltd.
30 Lesmill Road
Don Mills, Ontario, M3B 2T6, Canada

Distributed in Australia by
Peribo Pty Ltd.
58 Beaumont Road
Mount Kuring-gai, NSW 2080, Australia

Distributed in all other territories by
Grantham Book Services Ltd.
Isaac Newton Way, Alma Park Industrial Estate
Grantham, Lincolnshire, NG31 9SD, England

Library of Congress Cataloging-in-Publication Data is available upon request.

ISBN 1-55670-649-9

Printed in Singapore

10 9 8 7 6 5 4 3 2 1

Élisabeth Brami

Phillipe Bertrand

Little

Moments

of

Happiness

Translated by Alexandra Childs

Stewart, Tabori & Chang
New York

Watching the

full moon or

 a beautiful

sunrise together.

Gazing

at each

other without

blinking.

Holding

hands with

fingers

entwined.

Making

each other

lots of promises.

Telling each other
last night's dreams
every
morning over breakfast.

Dancing

like

crazy.

Talking late

into the night.

Remembering

something

before  leaving.

Running

 on a

beach.

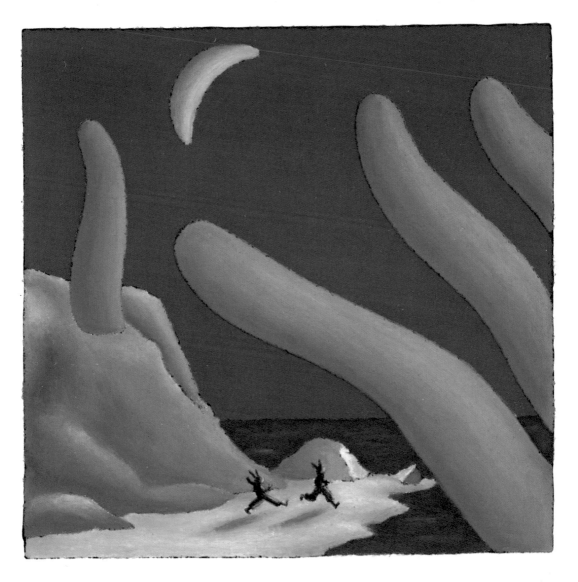

 Meeting

someone.

Saying something

that no one

else would

dare to say.

 Fighting.

Making

peace.

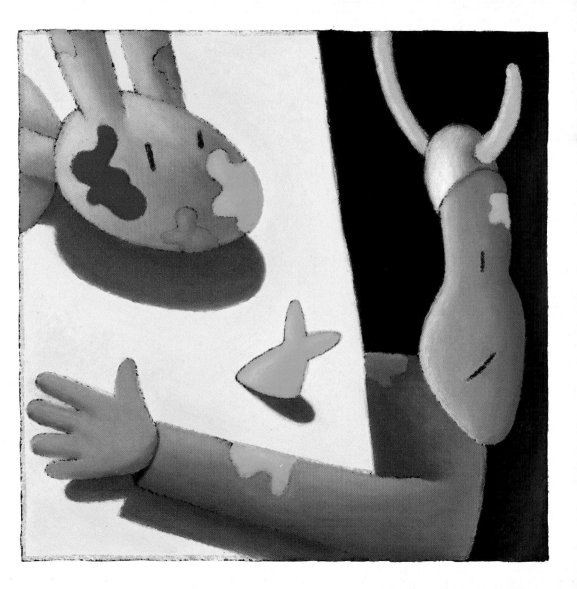

Giving someone a

drawing or

poem you made

yourself.

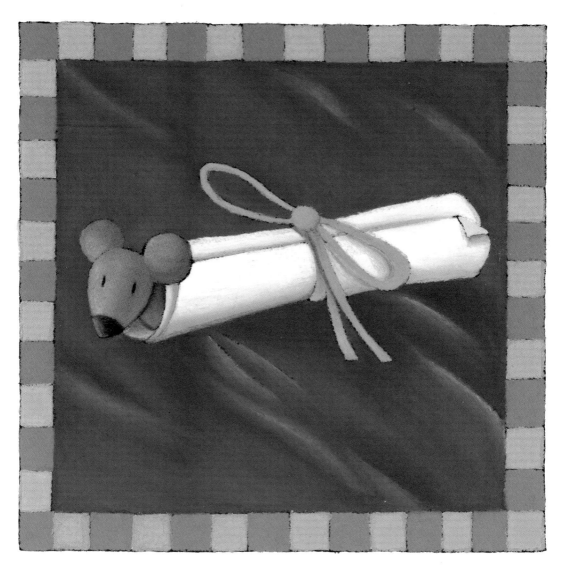

Sitting next to  each other

in silence.

Surprising

someone.

Getting ready

for a

date.

Discovering

 things

in common.

Closing your eyes,

face to face, then

 opening

them again.

Sharing

something

delicious

to eat.

Soaping

 each other's

back.

Waiting impatiently for a

phone call, 📞 a letter,

or the moment you see

each other again.

Kissing.

Snuggling up

to each

 other.

Finding dried flowers,

photos, or

 souvenirs and

remembering

someone you loved.

Strolling together
and talking about
 everything
and nothing.

Saying the same

word at

the same time.

Laughing your heads

off and

being the only ones

who know why.

Thinking of someone

and unexpectedly

 running

into them.

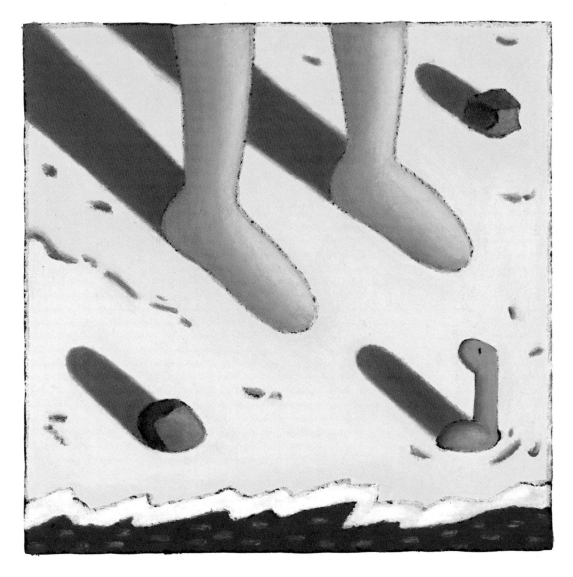

Loving someone

that you can't

put up with.

Having fun wearing

each other's

clothes.

Sleeping warmly

in the

arms of someone

you love.

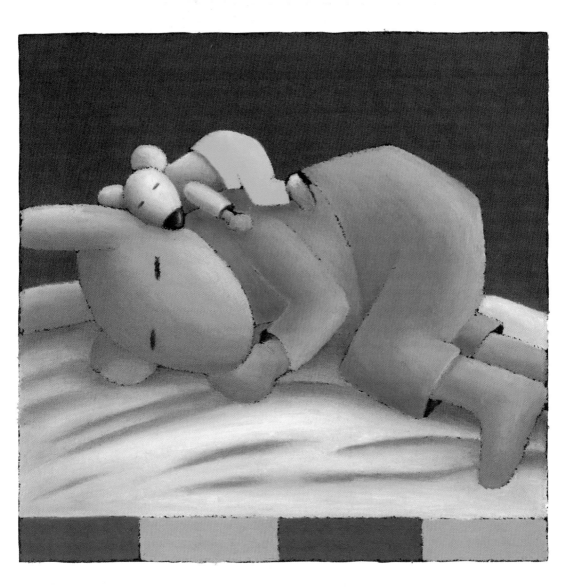